Advance

D0761483

"*Widowed Parents Unite* will be a comfort to any young widow who feels upended, overwhelmed, or isolated after this major life change. It's a collection of accessible stories and tips, a resource guide, and a trusted companion all rolled into one. Experienced, knowledgeable, and compassionate, Jenny Lisk is your perfect tour guide for this journey no one ever wants to take. She, and the voices of so many others, will help you feel less alone."

—HOPE EDELMAN, *New York Times* bestselling author of *Motherless Daughters* and *The AfterGrief: Finding Your Way Along the Long Arc of Loss*

"*Widowed Parents Unite* provides readers with the invaluable relief that accompanies having your fears, your truths, and your experiences validated. Jenny Lisk has brought together a diverse group of widowed parents to provide practical advice in short, easily digestible chapters that act as a light in the darkness for solo parents raising grieving kids. This book will accompany widowed parents as they craft a different life for themselves and their families."

—MICHELE NEFF HERNANDEZ, CEO,
Soaring Spirits International,
and author, ***Different After You:***
Rediscovering Yourself and
Healing after Grief and Trauma

"Grieving can be lonely business, but no matter how alone you might be feeling in your experience, *Widowed Parents Unite* offers hope, solace, comfort, and inspiration. Jenny Lisk has brought all the wisdom of her personal and professional experience to create a book full of tips, strategies, love, laughter, and the reminder that none of us have to walk through the dark all by ourselves."

—CLAIRE BIDWELL SMITH, LCPC,
author of ***Conscious Grieving***

"Sometimes in life when tragedy hits, people make lemonade from lemons. Jenny Lisk is doing just that as she continues to help other widows navigate grief. Grief is different for everyone, but knowing others' experiences seems to help when we're facing the unknown. *Widowed Parents Unite* is a book about community, written by community—and community helps healing. This book is filled with resources that you can refer to in the moment of your needs. The loudest message in this beautifully well-thought-out book is YOU ARE NOT ALONE! Get this book for yourself, and feel the love and support from others who have had similar experiences. Share this book as a gift when you don't know what to do or say to someone who is grieving."

—KAREN PHELPS MOYER, co-founder, Eluna Network, founder, Camp Erin, and life/love coach, Good Morning Gorgeous

"Jenny Lisk has written a book that is a balm for the aching soul. In a way, she has created a 'friend' in the form of a book that a widowed parent can turn to at any time of the day or night for guidance and support. You hear the real voices of surviving partners, one after another, providing bite-size nuggets of heart and wisdom. The writers come from all across the world and different cultures so there is something of value and relatability for everyone. Professionals who work with grieving parents will also benefit from reading the poignant messages that these brave widows and widowers have opened their hearts to contribute. This gem of a book is a resource to come to time and again."

—ELENA LISTER, MD, clinical associate professor of psychiatry and co-author of *Giving Hope: Conversations With Children About Illness, Death and Loss*

"Working with children and families experiencing grief over the last twenty-three years has taught me a lot. Jenny Lisk compiled all of these learnings into her book that will surely help so many. The common themes that resonated with me were the importance of community, highlighting communicating with your children about their feelings, and certainly showing your feelings to your kids. This is a gem for those who are solo parenting, as well as for those who work with grieving populations."

—RYAN LOISELLE, MSW, LICSW, program director, FRIENDS WAY, and founder, Rhode Island Grief Counseling

"Jenny Lisk's book, *Widow's Parents Unite*, offers an important promise of community at a time when most people feel their most isolated. An important voice of hope, practical support, and understanding to parents navigating the loss of a partner, this collection of short personal essays reminds us that grief deserves grace, that imperfect decisions made in the early throes of loss are not permanent, and that caretakers need community, too. This book will benefit anyone who reads it, and all of us if we take its wisdom to heart."

—MEGHAN RIORDAN JARVIS, MA, LICSW, host, *Grief is My Side Hustle* podcast, and author, *End of the Hour: A Therapist's Memoir*

"A jewel box of gems for widowed parents. Each weekly entry contains a precious gift of wisdom, insight, humanity, and above all, hope."

—JOANNE L. HARPEL, MPhil, CT, JD, president, Coping After Suicide, and executive producer, Talking OutLOUD: Teens & Suicide Loss, A Conversation

"*Widowed Parents Unite* is a manifesto for families learning how to navigate the griefall after loss. Keeping true to the idea that what works for one may not work for another, there are so many powerful perspectives on grief and the grief experience, that you will walk away feeling much less alone and more equipped to take another step forward, one moment at a time. This book needs to be in every school and community setting, and is an invaluable resource for anyone in the midst of a significant loss without knowing what comes next. I couldn't recommend this beautiful 'support system in a book' more!"

—GINA MOFFA, LCSW, grief and trauma therapist and author of *Moving On Doesn't Mean Letting Go: A Modern Guide to Navigating Loss*

"Once again Jenny Lisk provides widowed parents with an invaluable resource. This book is a great referral for therapists who work with anyone raising kids after the loss of their spouse or partner. *Widowed Parents Unite*, combined with Lisk's Widowed Parent Institute and the wealth of information found in her podcast interviews, don't take away widowed people's grief but do provide tremendous substantive support for them on their healing journey. This book is a testament to Lisk's impassioned desire to continue to serve the unfortunate few who find themselves parenting alone after losing their loved ones."

—CATHY CALLANS, LMHC,
St. Louise Counseling Services

Widowed Parents Unite

Widowed Parents Unite

52 Tips to Get Through the First Year,

from One Widowed Parent to Another

JENNY LISK

Bluhen
Books

For Nancy —
May you find solace in
community —
jll —
11.5. 2023

Widowed Parents Unite: 52 Tips to Get Through the First Year, from One Widowed Parent to Another

Bulk purchase inquiries: info@bluhenbooks.com
Speaking & interview requests: hello@jennylisk.com

ISBN: 978-1-7356136-4-2 (hardcover)
ISBN: 978-1-7356136-5-9 (paperback)
ISBN: 978-1-7356136-6-6 (ebook)

Library of Congress Control Number: 2023919004

Editing by Jocelyn Carbonara and Jenny Lisk
Cover design by David Provolo
Interior design by Jenny Lisk
Author photo by Danielle Barnum Photography

Published by Bluhen Books, Bellevue, Washington

For widowed parents everywhere:
May these stories shine for you
as a beacon of hope and practical wisdom

CONTENTS

Foreword

When I told my job interviewer in the hospital intensive care unit that I was no stranger to tragedy—having lost my father when I was a teen—little did I know that I was standing in the exact spot where my husband, Matthew Holt Redmond, would suddenly die of lung cancer complications just days later.

Shortly after I met Matthew in college, my discerning father announced that he was surely "the one" for me, and my mother enveloped him into our family. Matthew was studious, hardworking, respectful, faithful, and selfless. Months later, when my father abruptly passed away just after my nineteenth birthday, Matthew was unforgettably understanding of my grief journey and also went out of his way to help my widowed mother.

In our nine years together, my late husband and I traveled to more than thirty countries, worked in engineering internationally, wed in the US Virgin Islands, bought our first home on the side of Signal Mountain in Chattanooga, Tennessee, and blissfully expanded our family. Unfortunately, Matthew was diagnosed with early lung cancer while I was pregnant with our first son, Little Holt. After being declared cancer-free for over a year and a half, my beloved husband shockingly drew his last breath, hours after delivering a key work presentation, at age thirty-two. An acute oversight by his team of oncologists and specialists had cost him his life.

At just twenty-seven years old, I was a widow—five months pregnant, with our ten-month-old on my hip. My nurturing doula understood my conflicted joy as Little Holt took his first steps at Matthew's funeral. Soon after, my pregnancy became high-risk. As my health deteriorated, my loving mother Corinne Johnson became the bones of my spine. I wrestled with the anguish of losing my husband and the reality that I was losing my second pregnancy. Yet against all odds, I gave birth to Little Matthew.

Six months postpartum and three major surgeries later, my physical health was finally restored. My mental health, however, would take longer to revive. The weight of the world fell on my shoulders, and I was left with no answer to my most terrifying question: *What should I do now?*

I relied upon the esteemed and now-retired psychologist David Solovey, PhD, to guide me through my grief for many years. He suggested that I also seek a community of widowed parents for peer support.

That's when I stumbled upon *The Widowed Parent Podcast* by Jenny Lisk and received my first glimpse of a supportive widowed parent community. Later that night, as my little ones fell asleep listening to Jenny's soothing voice, tears streamed down my face. I realized I was not alone. Others were navigating parenthood through loss, and they were doing it together.

I learned that Jenny Lisk had started *The Widowed Parent Podcast* after her husband, Dennis, died of brain cancer. At the age of forty-three, she desperately wanted to know: *How exactly does someone raise grieving kids, anyway?*

Jenny set out to interview fellow widowed parents, people who had experienced early parent loss, and experts who could shed light on this question. She penned her first book, the award-winning memoir *Future Widow: Losing My Husband, Saving My Family, and Finding My Voice*. *Future Widow*, which quickly became one of my favorite books, also received accolades from children's grief experts, widowed parents, and grieving people the world over. It was even shared publicly by Katie Couric, who became a widowed parent of two young girls when her first husband died of a devastating colorectal cancer.

Most recently, Jenny founded the Widowed Parent Institute to bring clear, practical information, resources, and support to moms and dads who are raising grieving kids and teens. I only wish this much-needed resource had existed when my husband died.

As a widowed, solo parent, I have always been embraced by the love of both sets of grandparents, and after finding this podcast, I have been able to lean into the global widowed community as well. Leaders like Jenny Lisk helped me find my transformative passion. At the peak of the pandemic in 2020, just three years after Matthew's death, I stepped away from my background in engineering and founded the global nonprofit, Young, Black & Widowed Inc. To date, my organization has provided free peer grief support to more than 2,500 widows and widowers of every age, nationality, and religion worldwide. As I heal alongside our clients, it's an honor to be entrusted with the hearts of so many grieving people.

Today, six years post-loss, my profoundly autistic son and my neurotypical son are both gifted, thriving kindergarteners who love biking, kayaking, and camping with our service dog, Winter. Though my children were less than a year old when my husband passed, they still grieve. One of the most important points I learned from Jenny's podcast is that each time they reach a new developmental milestone, they will grieve the loss all over again, based on their greater understanding.

As I reflect on my experience, I'm pleased to introduce you to *Widowed Parents Unite: 52 Tips to Get Through the First Year, from One Widowed Parent to Another.* My hope is that it will expand the widowed parent support community, allowing more grieving parents to connect with one another as I once did. I also believe this book will serve as a resource and support tool for licensed mental health providers serving widowed parents—expanding on the important healing work with their clients.

I invite you to connect with the contributing authors and become involved with the collective efforts of Jenny Lisk's new Widowed Parent Institute. As you turn the page and meet our community, I trust you will find a reflection of your grief journey in our words of encouragement.

Azuráe Johnson Redmond
Founding director and certified grief coach,
Young, Black & Widowed Inc.

Introduction

I f you'd spotted us—four women in our forties, laughing, chatting, and drinking wine—you'd be forgiven for assuming we were merely busy parents, stressed-out professionals, or middle-aged girlfriends enjoying a quick getaway from the demands of everyday life.

We were, in fact, all of those things.

We were also widows.

In that charming tasting room in the Bavarian-inspired village of Leavenworth, Washington, I think we shocked the sommelier when, by way of making conversation, she inquired how we knew one another. The only answer we could muster was an unthinkable one: that each of our young husbands had died, leaving us widowed in our thirties and forties to raise our grieving kids alone.

Since you've picked up this book, I'm going to assume that you, too, have experienced the unimaginable: you've lost your spouse or partner, and now you're parenting solo.

I don't know if you're a mom or a dad, if your kids are young or if they're teens, if your loss was sudden and unexpected, or if it came after a long and difficult illness. But I do know this: widowed parenting is *hard*.

I'm so sorry you're living this nightmare.

Being a young widow can be lonely and isolating. I frequently hear from listeners of *The Widowed Parent Podcast* that they don't know anyone else in their neighborhood, school community, or personal circle who is widowed and now raising their kids or teens alone.

Sadly, however, there are a lot of us. Far too many, in fact.

Judi's House in Denver, which prepares the annual Childhood Bereavement Estimation Model, estimated in 2023 that one in twelve young people in the United States will lose a parent or sibling before they turn eighteen. Parent loss, it turns out, accounts for most of that number—so that's an awful lot of kids with a dead parent. Most of these kids will have a surviving parent, too—and that parent is *you*.

And—it's *me*.

Until my husband, Dennis, died when our kids were nine and eleven, I didn't know many younger widowed people. Sure, there was the mom whose husband died when our boys were in third grade together. I didn't know her well at the time, but I went to the funeral, and I dropped off a casserole when it was my turn on the meal train.

Then there was the woman whose husband died shortly after my son joined her son's Scout troop. But her kid was much older than mine, and we were brand new to the group, so I'd never met her. There was also my across-the-street neighbor—but her husband had died years earlier, before I met her, and somehow the topic of her dead husband never came up when we bumped into each other at our mailboxes.

And so it was that when I was widowed at the age of forty-three, I felt completely lost as a parent. I didn't know how to do this job—a job which I hadn't signed up for. Up to that point, my parenting experience had consisted primarily of "typical" kid issues—potty training, homework-wrangling, sibling rivalry, and the like—and I knew absolutely *nothing* about parenting grieving kids.

Perhaps that's where you're coming from too.

In fact, I'd wager that *most* of us who end up as widowed parents don't have any background or training in this area. We didn't get degrees in childhood psychology, develop expertise in grief and loss, or grow up with the devastation of being grieving children ourselves.

How then do we learn what we need to know?

One answer, I believe, is found in *community*. My own awareness of the importance of community for grieving people started when yet another neighbor, whose own husband had died five years earlier, reached out and introduced herself when Dennis was diagnosed with glioblastoma—an incredibly aggressive form of brain cancer with a single-digit survival rate. We walked a lot, and we talked a lot. Her presence and perspective were invaluable to me.

If you're not lucky enough—if we can even call it "lucky"—to have a widowed parent living across the street from you, another just around the corner, and a few others within a stone's throw, as I did, all is not lost. There are many other ways to tap into a community of people who "get it"—starting with this book.

The reflections and tips you'll find in these pages are offered in the spirit of reaching out a hand across time and distance to offer support and encouragement from each of us—the "seasoned" widowed parents who have contributed their wisdom to this book—to you, a newer widowed parent walking this path that none of us wishes we were on.

When I interview guests for my podcast, I always ask at the end: "If you could say one thing to widowed parents, what would it be?"

It's amazing how often the response is some variation of this essential message: "You are not alone."

I hope you'll see in the pages of this book that you also are not alone.

May these fifty-two tips and reflections, shared by your fellow widowed parents, bring you connection, support, and a small measure of comfort as you move forward on this path you didn't choose but upon which you find yourself nonetheless.

Week 1

Leslie Gray Streeter

I don't believe in one-size-fits-all tips, but this one's as close as you're gonna get: give yourself some grace.

Yes. I said it.

You.

The person holding it all together, even though that wasn't the plan. The one who is responsible for the mental, emotional, and financial well-being of all the people living in your house, and maybe a few who don't anymore. The strong one, who has to be all of everything to everyone.

Hold a little of that grace, that effort, that patience, for *you*.

You are going to get some things wrong.

But you are not a failure. This happened to you too. Breathe—and start from there.

Leslie Gray Streeter
Maryland, United States
Author, *Black Widow: A Sad-Funny Journey Through Grief for People Who Normally Avoid Books with Words Like "Journey" in the Title*

Week 2

Don Murray

After Gloria passed, I was devastated. It was during a long COVID lockdown, so I had to look after my two kids, then ages ten and fifteen, with no outside support.

I didn't know what to do, but I knew we needed some routine to keep us on track and bring us together. I pulled in an extra mattress and threw it onto the floor of my room, telling the kids we were all sleeping together in the same room. Each night, we would watch a movie together, and then all go to bed at the same time in the same room. I would also read a story to them when we were all in bed.

I think this joint family activity helped immensely. Having a routine, plus the sense of being a team and the "togetherness" we experienced, really helped us to get through those first few months. I told them they could sleep in my room as long as they wanted. Somewhere around four months in, the older teen started wanting to stay up later, which broke the cycle, and both kids gradually went back to their own rooms.

Looking back, I'm so glad we had this time together.

Don Murray
Victoria, Canada

Week 3

Laurel Beck

When my husband was diagnosed with cancer, he and I had to figure out when—and how much—to tell our son. I wanted to be honest and accurate in talking about the disease and treatment, in an age-appropriate way of course. Once it was clear the disease was terminal, we also talked about that with our son. Hospice was involved, including a wonderful social worker who met with our son during that time. We tried to cover his grief and emotional needs as best we could.

What I don't think I ever talked about, however, was what would happen to us after my husband died.

My son was thirteen when my husband died, and had a vivid imagination. The first night, when I dropped something on the floor, he came running up in a panic—clearly concerned that something had happened to me too.

It turned out that one of his biggest worries —which he eventually verbalized—was that we wouldn't be able to stay in our house and might need to live on the street. He also worried about whether he'd have to change schools, what we would eat, and whether I would stay healthy enough to take care of him. I wish I had started talking with him much sooner about the practical aspects of life after a parent dies. Once I realized my mistake, I did everything I could to make up for that void of information.

Laurel Beck
Washington, United States

Week 4

Viki Brown

My biggest tip for grieving parents is to humble yourself and accept help.

Allowing others to walk alongside you relieves you of responsibilities and allows others to feel like they are doing something.

Let them bring you dinner, let them clean your house, let them fix your washing machine.

Following Dustin's death, I had so many people wanting to help. It was hard at first to let them into my mess, but once I opened my home to them, I could truly breathe.

It gave me the time to be with my kids and not feel pulled in all directions by mundane tasks, and it let others feel like they were doing something.

Viki Brown
Indiana, United States
Founder, Dustin's Place

Week 5

Zaynab Ansari

Be kind to yourself. Remember this is a new life that you didn't want and that you never asked for, but it's the hand you were dealt.

There is an adjustment period for this new life. Take baby steps. Don't compare yourself to how you used to be or the way things were. Give yourself full permission to take things day by day, hour by hour, even minute by minute.

Time will slow down. Time will speed up. Don't beat yourself up if you're having a bad day, a bad week, or a bad month. You are strong and you are brave, even if you don't feel strong and brave.

You've been through the wringer, but you're still here—and you're still trying.

Zaynab Ansari
Tennessee, United States
Contributing author, *One Nation, Indivisible: Seeking Liberty and Justice from the Pulpit to the Streets*

Week 6

Rachel Kodanaz

I s it okay for your children to see you cry? Yes, of course. Expressing your sadness and emotions comes in various ways, and there is definitely a right time to cry in front of your children.

Crying is a natural emotional response that adults experience during sadness and grief, and it's important for children to understand that it's normal and healthy. When children see their parents cry, it provides an opportunity for them to learn about different emotions and how to cope with them. Crying helps children understand that everyone, including adults, experiences a range of emotions.

Also, witnessing their parents' vulnerability can help children express their own emotions, opening the door for greater communication and connection. However, it's crucial for parents to reassure their children that a parent's tears are not the child's fault and that they are loved and supported. It's essential to create an environment where children feel comfortable asking questions and expressing their emotions.

Rachel Kodanaz
Colorado, United States
Author, *Living with Loss, One Day at a Time*; *Finding Peace, One Piece at a Time*; and *Grief in the Workplace*

Week 7

Stephanie Nevins

My tip for a newly widowed parent is to accept early on that there are likely to be disorienting cognitive side effects of your grief.

I read that there are recent studies showing that the brain of a grieving person is actually "rewiring" itself on a grand scale—so there is a real reason you feel this way. For me, this looked like forgetfulness and a corresponding feeling that I was always neglecting to do something important.

So: Set up autopay for your bills ASAP. Create recurring reminders on your digital calendar for your kids' piano lessons and even for mundane events such as trash day. Consider reducing your cognitive load by accepting other parents' offers to bring your kids home from regularly scheduled activities like soccer practice, or by putting your living room lamps on timers so you don't have to turn them off before bedtime. Every little thing helps.

Most importantly, give yourself a lot of grace for missing the really obvious things that will, nevertheless, somehow slip through the cracks.

Stephanie Nevins
Illinois, United States

Week 8

Joe Basile

After my wife passed away from cancer and our two boys lost their mom, my older son, who was nine at the time, said to me after one of his counseling sessions, "I never thought of you as a parent."

Initially, this knocked the wind out of me. I couldn't believe it because I had always shown my love and support for him, and the two of us had plenty of fun, one-on-one, father-son experiences together.

It took me a while to realize what he meant by "parent." You see, before my wife died, my primary focus was on being the breadwinner of the family, whereas my wife was a full-time mom who took the lead on all decisions and activities for the boys. Whenever they needed support or help in any way, they would always go to their mom first. Afterward, if needed, I might be brought in to add my perspective.

After her death, it took some time to adjust to my "new normal" as the sole parent responsible for their emotional, physical, and financial well-being. In this role, the most important lesson I've learned is to reassure them of the following: they can talk to me about anything, I'll always love them unconditionally, I'll accept them for who they are, I'm proud of them, and I'll support them in all their endeavors.

Joe Basile
Oregon, United States

Week 9

Nicole Antich

E xcept where you may not have a choice, give yourself as much grace and time as possible to make any major life decisions.

When my husband passed away, I felt I needed to move from our large house into a small apartment right away. In doing so, I purged a lot of his and my belongings before I was really ready. There are a lot of things I wish I would have kept, but everything felt so urgent at the time—like I needed to get it all done right away to get my life in order. I wish I would have given myself more time to make those decisions when my head was clearer.

Nicole Antich
Washington, United States

Week 10

Sandra Began

It was the first week of school when my husband died by suicide. My son Jack was starting seventh grade at a new school, and my son Charlie was starting third grade.

The week after my husband died, I made appointments with the principal, psychologist, counselor, and every one of their teachers. I took a friend with me and met with all of them. I told them my husband died by suicide and I needed their help to watch out for any signs of emotional distress my boys may have.

I wanted the teachers and administrators to be honest and transparent with me if my boys were struggling in school. Many of them thanked me for giving them the opportunity to help my children and their friends, and said they wished more parents met with them after the death of a loved one so they could give the children better support.

Sandra Began
Connecticut, United States
Founder, The Widow Project

Week 11

Ashley Humbyrd

After my husband died, some very well-intentioned people thought they knew what was best for me. I heard, "Go back to work. It will take your mind off things," and, "You can't lie in bed. Doing things will make you feel better."

I really didn't need their judgment and wish I had tuned them out, since I just ended up feeling worse. My mental health suffered as I started putting on a performance to please others, and I completely burned out.

The reality is that people deal with loss differently, and there's no right way or wrong way to grieve. Loss brings a time of adjustment which is painful and far from pretty. Don't let anyone guilt you into things you aren't ready for. If you need to take more time off work, take it. If you need a daily nap, take it. Dishes are piling up and you can't remember the last time you vacuumed? Not a problem. As long as your child's needs are being met, you're doing just fine. Your kid will be okay in front of the TV for a while as you give yourself what you need.

Take the word "should" out of your vocabulary, and do what's necessary to get yourself through those first months.

Ashley Humbyrd
Rhode Island, United States

Week 12

Carole Marie Downing

Be open to moments of joy.

Grief can be all-consuming—a gray blanket as thick and endless as a Pacific Northwest winter sky. But even cloudy days have moments of sunshine.

Those few rays of light streaming between the clouds don't change the weather, but they can be just enough to hold out hope for the brighter days of summer. Small moments of joy can serve the same purpose in grief.

I remember at one point thinking that if I could just string together enough moments of joy, I would someday feel happy again. A moment of delight with my son learning how to blow a bubble for the first time, my dog running ecstatically on the beach, the relief of laughter with a good friend, or a song on the radio that made me dance, even just a little—these tiny moments led me through the gray days of grief and brightened life just enough to help me continue through the darkness.

Let joy in. Grief will return, as grief does, but you will not be betraying grief when you feel the relief of joy. Be on the lookout for those moments of joy, as they light the way to a new life after loss.

Carole Marie Downing
Oregon, United States
Author, *Singing Beyond Sorrow: A Year of Grief, Gratitude, and Grace*

Week 13

Maya Etienne

R emember that you cannot be both Mom and Dad.

Seeking help to fill the gaps in your kids' lives resulting from the death of their other parent takes courage, but it's worth it. Figure out where your kid needs additional support, and seek out friends, family, and programs that can step up to help.

Remember that no one person will be able to fill the shoes of the parent who died, but a group of people can help and guide your kids in different parts of their lives. Be flexible in the support you receive, and know that it may not always be the same set of people mentoring your kid over time. The important part is that your kids are surrounded by caring adults who have their best interests at heart.

Maya Etienne
Indiana, United States
Grief Companion

Week 14

Daniela Goldfine

When you become widowed, people will talk, give advice, and suggest a million different things. They are just trying to help, but generally they are clueless.

Unless they have gone through your specific experience, which is a rare occurrence, the road ahead is just yours. There is no roadmap, there are no guidelines, and you are figuring this out for yourself and your children.

However, it's important to remember that other people can be there for you: family, friends, colleagues, your kids' teachers, neighbors, and so many others. You are allowed to choose who is helpful (and not) at any given time during the first year(s); do not feel guilty about this.

As the sole parent of your kids, you are now making every decision. It is overwhelming, but it is the only way forward. You've got this.

Daniela Goldfine
Minnesota, United States

Week 15

David Kelly

I found my sense of achievement crushed in early widowhood. I went from someone who'd always been productive in activities to someone who was overcome with apathy and lack of motivation. In grief, I was always feeling like a complete failure by not being able to accomplish most of what I could readily complete prior to widowhood.

I learned to be kinder to myself and to reframe my achievement toward something more realistic given my circumstances. Instead of one giant to-do list, I started to create a daily, more feasible "three things to-do list" on a Post-It note.

Having a smaller, more manageable list that

was achievable helped me to not exhaust my reduced levels of motivation and to regain a sense of accomplishment each day.

David Kelly
London, United Kingdom

Week 16

Karen Paul

My husband spent fifty-four weeks battling terminal brain cancer and died in our home. I was his twenty-four-hour caretaker while also supporting our three teenage children in their fear and anger.

When he was sick, our children stopped congregating in family spaces, spending most of their time in their rooms behind closed doors. After he died, I knew that my first job, even in the midst of my own grief, was to work to bring joy and laughter back into our home.

And I knew that for us that meant getting a dog. So we adopted Bo. And my children came out of their rooms and spent all their time hugging and loving the new member of our family.

It's true what they say about rescues: we rescued him, and he indeed rescued us.

Karen Paul
Maryland, United States

Week 17

Elke Thompson

B e honest. Don't try to make death sound "nicer." Don't say things like, "She has gone to sleep," or "He has gone to a better place."

I know you are trying to protect your kids, but unfortunately you are not doing so by pretending that everything is okay when it really isn't. And by using metaphors—rather than simple-to-understand language like, "Her heart has stopped beating, and she died"—you can even have the opposite effect and cause deep emotional upset and panic attacks. This may cause your child to wonder: *Will I die if I go to sleep? Will you? What did I do to make him go away?*

I know it's not easy, but talking to your children honestly is the best way you can support and help them right now.

Elke Thompson
Scotland, United Kingdom
Speaker and children's book author
Is Daddy Coming Back in a Minute?
What Happened to Daddy's Body?
Is It Still OK to Have Cuddles?

Week 18

Tonia Wilson

It's hard to imagine being a widow at thirty-four, and even harder being a solo parent. How would I make sure my son felt the love of two parents after one died? Raised by women myself, how could I raise my son alone? These were some of the questions I asked myself.

I counted on my family and friends to help but never considered that they all had their own lives. I had to create a support team: babysitters, emergency contacts, mentors, etc. I went through various babysitters until I found one that fit my needs. And I was grateful to find a male mentor for my son through the Big Brothers Big Sisters program.

Know that the support system you set up might change several times, and that's okay.

Don't get overwhelmed when you hear "no;" in the words of my late friend Lorrie, one "no" doesn't stop the show.

Creating a new support system can be overwhelming initially, but you'll feel accomplished once you've it set up. Accept that plans will change, and get used to adapting. Show yourself grace while you're under the pressure of solo parenting. Know that you're doing the best you can. No "best parent" award exists. Kids need love, not perfection, and love doesn't cost anything but your time. Keep moving forward; you've got this.

Tonia Wilson
Michigan, United States
Cohost, *Conversations Between Widows* Podcast

Week 19

Leila Salisbury

Those who have grieved will understand that sometimes grief, especially early grief, can be so raw that your body actually hurts. This is one of the more obvious signs pointing to the deep connections between the mind and body, and between mental health and your physical level of wellness.

So to get us through the painful first year after our loss, I started acupuncture and monthly massage therapy. I introduced my daughter, who was also having a number of physical manifestations of her grief, to Jin Shin Jyutsu (a form of acupressure), yoga, and massage therapy. For both of us, these evolved into practices with emotional freedom technique (EFT) tapping and Jin Shin Jyutsu that we still call upon when moments of grief resurface.

Being aware of the grief in our bodies helped open both of us to being much more mindful of, and open to, the other parts of our grief.

Leila Salisbury
Kentucky, United States
Founder, Kentucky Center for Grieving Children and Families

Week 20

Marny Williams

Every parent worries about their children's well-being, and this worry only increases after the death of our kids' other parent.

We wonder if they will be okay and how their parent's death might impact their future. The reality is that we don't know. Kids, just like adults, have their own unique ways of expressing grief. And if we have more than one child, each will have their own unique style of grieving. Some may be quiet and it may feel like they aren't grieving at all, while others are more vocal or animated.

As a parent, what can we do to help? Grieving isn't easy, but I always tried to model healthy grief in my home. Healthy grief is emotional and messy, and requires us to ask for help, learn new coping strategies, and build a network of support around us.

We want to make the conversation of grief a safe topic in our homes. If our kids see us being authentic, talking about our partner, and honoring our emotions, then they will know they can come to us when they are ready to do the same.

Marny Williams
Waterloo, Canada
Founder, Hummingbird Centre for Hope

Week 21

Gary Ireland

I n the immediate months following the passing of my wife, Nancy, I quickly realized that, while I was grieving, I was also being watched closely by my kids. I also realized that I needed more time to grieve. Because I am in recovery, I was frequently asked to speak at meetings in the immediate months following her passing. This helped me to feel I was helping others who may be going through something similar, or at least encouraging them to stay in recovery. I also joined a grief group at Red Door (formerly Gilda's Club). I found comfort in speaking to others, reaching out, and hopefully helping when and if I could.

I also focused on all the immediate tasks at home: making sure the kids had health care, including psychological care, getting them reenrolled in school, and taking care of the many, many daily jobs that Nancy regularly had taken care of in our relationship. I remember once, in a lighter moment, when saying to my daughter yet again, "That was generally something Mommy would take care of," she jokingly replied, "Dad, you always say Mom took care of 'it'—whatever 'it' is. What exactly did *you* do around here?" We both laughed!

I've found that when I'm trying to help others—whether other grieving people, my own children, or anyone else —I'm able to step outside my own grief for a bit.

Gary Ireland
New York, United States

Week 22

Kali Sakai

I was utterly depleted after my husband's battle with cancer and had done little to keep up my own health. After he died, I finally prioritized my own wellness.

Addressing wellness will look different for everyone. It can include a more singular focus or a combination of things like counseling, bereavement support groups, massage, acupuncture, naturopathy, chiropractic care, fitness classes, yoga, personal training, physical therapy, spa treatments—anything that is rejuvenating and rebuilding.

I know I can't be the mom I want to be for my kids if I'm spent and unraveling. The work I did (and continue to do) with my wellness team fills me up with gratitude and shows me how capable I am of being a present and supportive solo parent.

Kali Sakai
Washington, United States

Week 23

Jen Zwinck

Widowed parenting is the hardest job in the world.

My number one piece of advice is this: be an example for your kids. By that I mean show that you're sad, show that you're angry, show that you're frustrated with the hand you've been dealt. Cry with them, hug them, hold them. Grieve together. But then pick yourself up, dust yourself off, and show your kids that you're okay. Be that example of strength. They need to feel that safety and security from you as their only parent left.

Also show them that you can still be happy, you can still find joy in life, and that you still have so much to live for and look forward to. Show them that you will make the best of this new life, and that you're going to do it together! That balance of what they see in you will guide them for the rest of their lives.

Jen Zwinck
Louisiana, United States
Host, *Widow 180: The Podcast*
Cofounder, The Widow Squad

Week 24

Azuráe Johnson Redmond

Our first son took his first steps at ten months old at my late husband's graveside service. It was a breezy, summer day in Tennessee as I walked numbly along the headstones of his extended family in their historic church cemetery. I was only twenty-seven years old and five months pregnant with our second son.

As my ten-month-old son greeted every friend and family member throughout the memorial service with a glowing, toothless grin, many commented how fortunate my two young sons were that they would never have to suffer through the grief of losing their father. After all, they were far too young to grieve; our second son was still in the womb. Yet at each developmental milestone, my sons grieved as they matured and gained more understanding of their loss.

Open, positive, age-appropriate communication across our entire extended family about losing their father to lung cancer was key, but it was complicated by the profound, low-verbal autism of one of my sons. My gifted special needs son would turn four before learning to use assistive technology well enough to communicate any feelings at all. Now in kindergarten together, my sons excitedly ask questions and happily swipe through thousands of digital photographs and handwritten journal entries from my late husband's accomplished yet short life as a full-time, international, professional engineer and hang glider pilot hobbyist.

Widowed parents: though painful in the very beginning, keep the bright memory of your late spouse alive for your children with stories told firsthand by you, grandparents, and friends.

Azuráe Johnson Redmond
Tennessee, United States
Nonprofit founder and certified grief coach,
Young, Black & Widowed Inc.

Week 25

Kelly Chavez

The tip that I've learned is that it's okay to say no.

My husband, Marty, was a stay-at-home dad who was constantly on the go with our kids. After he died, I felt like I had to keep up that same level of energy. I learned over time that not only was this unsustainable for me, but it also wasn't necessary. I learned to evaluate what was really needed or wanted, and then make decisions about where to put my energy.

As an example, at Christmas I sat down with my kids and asked for their top traditions that they felt were special about Christmas. I learned that we needed to decorate, but we didn't have to go crazy or over-the-top. I learned that decorating sugar cookies was important to them, for example, but that I could buy the premade cookies and icing.

I also learned to outsource. I took a hard look at my "to do" list and figured out what jobs I wanted to keep and which ones others could do (even if it meant paying people). Learning to say no helped me to feel less burned out and more able to have fun with my family and my friends.

Kelly Chavez
Washington, United States

Week 26

Kim Murray

The biggest mistake I made as a widowed solo parent was making everything my kids did or said mean something about me as a parent. When they were good, I was a good parent. When they did something bad, I was a terrible parent. And when my son stared me down with his steely eyes and hissed in my face that he wished I was dead? Worst parent of the year!

It took me a long time and a lot of therapy to realize my kids were separate individuals with their own thoughts and feelings. Every self-help guru claimed my kids' responses meant more about them than they did about me. My parenting wasn't lacking. It was my own *thoughts about myself as a parent* that caused all my problems. Parenting became a whole lot easier when I stopped taking my kids' behavior personally. I instead decided I was a stellar parent doing the best she could under some really crappy circumstances.

Kim Murray
Michigan, United States
Cofounder, The Widow Squad

Week 27

Craig Davis

One of the greatest pieces of advice I've received during this journey is to communicate with your kids. It's so important that they understand they need to communicate with you as well. You can facilitate this communication by sharing your feelings and thoughts, and if you have young children, reading children's books about loss and grief with them.

Bedtime can be extremely difficult, and children's books about loss and grief are so helpful to steer conversation and ease sleepy and tired minds at the end of the day. Always —always—pre-read these books so you know how you will react while sharing them. Know that children's movies can be tricky too, because many seem to have a storyline that includes a dead or dying parent.

Craig Davis
Indiana, United States

Week 28

Katie O'Brien

A friend in my caregiver support group introduced me to "cave days," which became some of my favorite days. Cave days are solo days, just for you, to do anything you want: sleep, read, eat chips in bed—anything! It's easy; just crawl into your "cave" and let the world (and your kids) carry on without you for as long as you can manage to keep them away. Plan it ahead of time, follow through, and enjoy the accomplishment of excellent self-care.

Katie O'Brien
Washington, United States

Week 29

Lucy Lloyd

My girls were very young when they lost their dad. They seem to take a lot of comfort in hearing me remember him aloud: "This reminds me of the time that Dad…" or "Dad used to love that…." Usually I just get little anecdotes or memories that pop into my mind anyway, and I make a point of sharing them.

The girls also like hearing specific ways they are like him. Whether it's activities they like, foods they hate, school subjects they enjoy, favorite songs, or aspects of their appearance, they appreciate when I draw similarities between them and their dad. It helps them get to know him better.

My older daughter even made three lists

one day: "Ways I am like Dad," "Ways I am like Mom," and "Ways I am like Both." My youngest has very few of her own memories of him; she was only two at the time he died. She has taken a lot of comfort in seeing pictures of just the two of them, affirming that he was there, she did know him, he did love her, and that they did have time together, even though she may not remember it. I made a book out of those pictures, and we titled it the *Margaret & Dad Book*. She looks at it often and takes it places, and it has helped her.

Lucy Lloyd
Kentucky, United States

Week 30

Pamela Addison

Birthdays, anniversaries, holidays, and other special occasions are difficult as a widowed parent.

When we reach one of those days, I have made it our new tradition to do something Papa would have loved. The best part of this is that we have so much fun, and we know Papa is right there in our hearts.

To see my children's beautiful smiles and hear their infectious laughter, I know they have not only done something that would have put a huge smile on their Papa's face, but also that we are making one of his dreams become a reality.

That makes those days a little bit easier to handle.

Pamela Addison
New Jersey, United States
Founder, Young Widows and Widowers of
COVID-19
Certified grief educator

Week 31

Mae Yoshikawa

As we approached my husband's death anniversary, our eleven-year-old son was hit with a fresh tsunami of grief.

"I miss Daddy. Mom, why did he have to die? Why did he have to die?" He repeated in agony.

I nestled beside him. If there's anything I've learned from my grief, it's that these emotions need to be allowed—free to be as they are, and free to move out.

I stroked his back. "What an awesome child you are, just as you are. All of your feelings are important."

But his grief surged stronger.

"I want to die, Mom. Can you kill me?"

I knew this thought all too well. So I

allowed this thought. I did not ask him to be another way. Why resist something that is, in the moment, real to him? My job is to love him regardless of anything, including uncomfortable emotions. Holding him, I felt my heart fill with silent prayers.

Often it's easier to resist or deny such feelings as in, "Don't say that," or, "Shh. You won't always feel this way." But in my experience, when I'm not present with what comes up in the moment, something will *feel off*, and ultimately this *won't work*. Dodging these emotions would be like dodging a part of my son. In this way, I learned the true value of holding space. Astonishingly, this has wildly expanded my capacity for grace. I know my son feels it too.

Mae Yoshikawa
Tokyo, Japan
Author, *Kizuki: Life's Tidal Waves + Epiphanies = Love Beyond Time and Death* (forthcoming)

Week 32

Will Owens

For widowed fathers who may not have been completely "plugged into" their young children's social and school circles prior to the deaths of their wives, widowed parenting can be especially tough.

I've learned that the moms of your children's friends can be your biggest allies. If you do not know them well, you should befriend them now. Trust me, they know the dates for the soccer registration deadline, the school field trip, and the teacher's birthday. They can help with carpool, playdates, and summer camps.

Though it may feel a little weird at first, join the "moms" Facebook group at the elementary school, sign up for their email distribution list, and join or start a group text thread with the mothers of five or six of your child's closest friends. They can be your saviors on many occasions.

Will Owens
North Carolina, United States

Week 33

Marisela Marquez

There are several things that I wish I had known about grief ahead of time—before I hit rock bottom.

What stands out for me is the importance of mourning our grief. I had what one might call "grief overload." I had experienced multiple significant losses in a short amount of time, and I didn't know how to mourn my grief. Instead, I avoided and suppressed my grief at all costs.

I also had difficulty finding local, relatable resources for young widows. I felt utterly lost in the world, and my sorrow consumed me to the point where I attempted to take my life.

Many research studies reflect the importance of paying attention to our grief. Avoiding and suppressing it can only take us so far before it comes out in other ways.

Marisela Marquez
Arizona, United States
Host, *The Embracing Widowhood Podcast*
Author, *The Magical Soul*, *El Alma Mágica*, and *I Love You Always & Forever / Siempre te voy amar* (children's books)

Week 34

Belinda Faught

I only recently started to understand what it means when people say you need to "do the work' in grief—but you do.

Do the minimum you must do to get by, and don't worry about anything else. Outsource as much as possible, and accept all help from friends and family. Be super kind to yourself, and don't expect to "grieve to a timetable;" it's gonna hurt like hell for longer than society deems acceptable. Go gently and stay away from the news, social media, and anything or anyone that doesn't serve you.

Find a fellow widow to hang out with in real life if you can; only they can truly under-stand what it's like. Meditate, move your body, journal, breathe, and try to strip life back to its essentials as much as possible.

I don't know that loss ever gets easier, but with time you'll eventually learn to carry your grief differently.

Belinda Faught
Sydney, Australia

Week 35

Marketta Davis

My husband passed when I was six weeks pregnant with our first baby. Even in the aftershock, I began orchestrating ways to turn his items into priceless keepsakes for myself and for our child. Turning his T-shirts into quilts, transforming his military uniforms into stuffed bears, molding shells from his twenty-one gun salute into crosses—I was constantly thinking of ways to conceptualize our fairytale life into material possessions. My most prized creation: our daughter's "Daddy Doll."

In 2001, when my husband and I had just started dating, he bought me a recordable photo frame. Included with his high school senior portrait was his voice: "Hey, beautiful! I just want to tell you that I love you. I always will, forever, and even after that. This way I can tell you when I'm not even there." That message was recorded eighteen years ago, as if he knew he'd leave me one day, too soon, with this beautiful little girl to whom I'd gift a plushy doll featuring a full-length photo of her dad in his Air Force blues and his recorded message inside—a message that could easily have been meant just for her.

The first year after losing a spouse is a blur of mixed emotions that can devastate any happy memories you had from a life so unfairly snatched from you. Hold fast to those you can remember by setting aside items you can memorialize in some unique way when the time allows.

Marketta Davis
Florida, United States
Board member, Young, Black & Widowed Inc.

Week 36

Melissa Gould

There is nothing harder than being a widowed parent. NOTHING. I prefer to refer to our group as "only parents"—as in, *I have an only child, and I am now an only parent.* Not a single parent, not a solo parent, an ONLY parent.

I have found that it's important to remember that we all grieve in our own way, and one isn't better or worse than any other. My daughter and I grieved so differently! I told the world; she didn't want to discuss it. I had to learn to be okay with that.

It's been many years since we lost my husband/her father, and we're in a much better place with our grief. We've both made room for it. Grief is a constant companion, but it's not nearly as heavy as it was in the early days of our loss. My daughter is now a young adult, and she's doing great! Our lives are full and happy, and Joel is never far from either of our thoughts.

Melissa Gould
California, United States
Author, *Widowish*

Week 37

Chase Jacobson

Remember what your role is to your children. I am a father, and it was tough for me to try to be both the father and the mother. When I tried to fill both roles, it was extremely frustrating. This set me up for failure, as I could never be the mother that my late wife had been to our children. Once I accepted that I could not be both father and mother to our kids, my overall confidence as a parent and quality of life improved dramatically. These changes were reflected in how my children responded to me.

Chase Jacobson
North Carolina, United States

Week 38

Lynn Haraldson

When my husband Bruce died, our daughter was only eleven days old, and my relationship with my in-laws wasn't great. Fortunately, Bruce's parents later worked with me to create an amicable relationship so that my daughter—their granddaughter—could grow up as part of their family too.

I realize that sometimes it's not in the surviving parent's or child's best interest to maintain a relationship with their partner's family. Barring serious issues, however, I encourage widowed parents to maintain a relationship with at least one person in their late partner's family, even if that requires putting aside past differences. In my experience, children need to feel part of both their parents' families—and what's a better way to get to know your deceased parent than by hearing the stories that only their family members can tell?

Some people might hesitate to talk about the person who died, either because they think it will upset the children or because of their own grief. It's been such a gift for my daughter, however, to grow up surrounded by the love and memories of her entire family, because Bruce's parents and I worked together to maintain that connection.

Lynn Haraldson
Pennsylvania, United States
Author, *An Obesity of Grief: A Journey from Traumatic Loss to Undying Love*

Week 39

Melissa Pierce

Y ou're solo parenting, which means you are doing everything to keep your family afloat: working to pay bills, grocery shopping, helping with homework, carpooling, housework, preparing meals—the list of "things to do" is endless.

The first thing on that to-do list should be YOU. Prioritizing yourself and taking care of your needs is absolutely essential to your physical and emotional health.

Choose to carve out some time just for you to replenish your energy. It could be going for a walk, soaking in a warm bath, talking with a close friend, spending some quiet time journaling or in meditation.

The ways in which you can care for yourself are countless, and you are worth it!

Melissa Pierce
Oregon, United States
Author, *Filled with Gold: A Widow's Story*
Cofounder, The Widow Squad
Cohost, *The Widow Squad Podcast*

Week 40

Marjorie Brimley Hale

W hen people would ask me what it was like to live with my father after being widowed, I would often say that it was wonderful to have my dad around. "He's a saint!" I said, and everyone agreed. What other seventy-year-old man would move in with his daughter and help raise her kids? He potty-trained the youngest, taught the eight-year-old math, and played baseball with the middle kid.

But the thing was, this process wasn't always smooth. Sometimes our parenting styles would differ, sometimes we hated the food the other person made, and sometimes I got tired of his piles all over the house.

I guess the thing that kept us together and made our mutual lives work was that we really tried to see things from the other person's viewpoint. I knew his body hurt more than mine when he spent hours on the floor playing Legos, and he knew I was tired when I got home from work. This knowledge let us be more gentle with each other than we might have been otherwise.

Really, I think we were able to do this because we understood each other's pain. He knew what it was like to grieve like I was grieving, since he'd been widowed himself at the age of fifty. And I understood what he'd been through as well.

Marjorie Brimley Hale
Washington, DC, United States
Writer, *DC Widow Blog*

Week 41

Kali Sakai

While we have pictures of my late husband throughout the house, I also borrowed a tradition from my Asian heritage and created a special area dedicated to remembering him.

I repurposed an end table and decorated it with photos, mementos, tchotchkes, a tiny urn with some of his ashes, an electric timer candle that lights up at random times, and a book of stories and thoughts about him from friends and family.

That was also where we hung his stocking on our first Christmas, since the table was near our fireplace.

This honors his continued presence in our lives and gives us a place to look or focus when we are thinking of him throughout the day.

Kali Sakai
Washington, United States

Week 42

Raju Panjwani

The words I didn't want to hear when my wife died—and frankly, still don't want to hear today—were these: "Time will heal." These are just words from someone who can only imagine your pain. We all know that we cannot truly understand anyone else's pain or experience.

What did help me was diving wholeheartedly into my wife's care. With her end inevitable from the first day of her diagnosis, I wanted to live fully with her each day. The boys became part of my care team and helped clean wounds, empty bags hanging from her body, manage IVs, and dispense medicines. While none of those things could possibly erase that nagging about-to-lose-her feeling, or heal our grief when we subsequently lost her, I'm so glad we could spend this time together.

My main tip is this: be fully present in your own journey. Let your children experience their own journeys too. We attended a grief support program at Tree House in Westchester County, New York, whose tagline says it all: "You are not alone." My younger son and I benefited greatly from this program, which allowed him to spend time with other kids who had lost a parent, and me to get to know other widowed adults.

Raju Panjwani
South Carolina, United States

Week 43

Karen Paul

My husband's closest band of friends, all amazing dads themselves, really wanted to offer themselves as surrogate fathers to our youngest son after my husband died. But at fourteen, my son was not interested. After a while, our friends stopped thinking about how to help. Yet I knew that someday their offer to invest love and time would pay off.

And it has; just this week, my now twenty-year-old son is reaching out to one of those dads for help and support, knowing that our friend is loving and trustworthy, and as good a "dad replacement" as possible.

Be patient; everyone in grief has their own timeline. You can put in place the building blocks for support, knowing that children especially will know when it's the right time to reach out for help.

Karen Paul
Maryland, United States

Week 44

Jeanette Koncikowski

It's important to remember that our grief can coexist with other emotions and experiences. We shouldn't chastise ourselves for finding joy or happiness wherever we can while we are bereaved.

As you learn to cope with everything, you'll grow through your grief. In some ways, this may feel like it's taking you further and further from your loved ones, but the person you are now, this survivor, deserves good things too. When you do the hard work of grieving, joy is right on the other side. You just have to reach out and claim it.

If I've taken anything away from my loss, it's that my life is important too, and I get to define what my life after loss looks like.

Jeanette Koncikowski
New York, United States
Author, *Shipwrecked: A Memoir on Widowed Parenting* (forthcoming)

Week 45

Pamela Addison

Despite the pain and heartache you feel now, finding the joy in life is a worthy pursuit. It's what helped me get through my first year of widowed parenthood.

I wanted my children to continue to have as much happiness and joy in their lives as they did before losing my husband. To see their smiles and hear their laughter helped heal my heart and let me move forward with our lives.

I discovered that in finding the joy in life, I was also honoring my husband's life, because all he ever wanted in this world was for us to be happy.

It's not always easy to find that joy, but when you do, it is totally worth it!

Pamela Addison
New Jersey, United States
Founder, Young Widows and Widowers of COVID-19
Certified grief educator

Week 46

Elizabeth Colby Davie

B e very kind, gentle, and patient with yourself. This is not just the loss of a single person, but the loss of life as you knew it. Your thoughts and feelings may be all over the place for some time, and you will need to gradually build a life around your loss, not just "get through it."

For me, the first flickers of joy in my widowed life came when I began taking ceramics classes. Over two years, I progressed from an uninformed beginner to being able to make mugs and bowls that I loved. Other people enjoyed them too.

My new hobby has taken me to unfamiliar towns and buzzing studios, introduced me to creative and kind people, and opened an entire world for me. It has given me hope and energy. The beauty of the colored glazes on my fired, finished pieces and the solid evidence of my improved skill never fail to cheer me up.

When you feel stuck, try learning something new. Your children will notice and thrive when you spark with enthusiasm for life again. Even if you don't think it's possible now, you will find that spark again.

Elizabeth Colby Davie
Massachusetts, United States

Week 47

Angel Larrauri

I talked with my kids six months after my wife died to see how they would feel if I met a "special friend." I wasn't dating anyone at the time, but this discussion helped plant the seed for my future happiness. Before starting a new relationship, I decided it was important that any future partner feel comfortable with my kids and me talking openly of the stories, jokes, and experiences we'd shared with "Mama" and "Lizz."

About a year and a half later, I reconnected with an old friend from my hometown—someone I'd known since middle school. After a year of visiting and talking over the phone, we got married, and today we are blessed with much happiness. My new wife loves my kids, and the fact that she and I have known each other since 1981 has made things easier for me. She is now focused on developing a relationship with my kids, as she hadn't previously known them. My new wife also respects our memories of my late wife and always seeks to learn about our happy moments with her, which has been helpful for all of us.

Angel Larrauri
Virginia, United States

Week 48

Marni Henderson

When I hear from adults who, during their youth, lost a parent, all too often they tell me how important they felt it was that their other parent "keep living." *Living* in this case means that the parent remained present with them—the children—while still engaging in life. Many felt instead that their surviving parent had emotionally died with the other parent.

As adults, we understand that, yes, a part of us did die with our partner—yet we are still alive, our children are watching, and they need us now more than ever to be authentic, present, and engaged adults. We must tend to our personal well-being with fierce diligence, which includes the active process of grieving, healing, growing, *and* learning to create new life. This requires taking the steps necessary to nurture ourselves in ways we may never have done before. As we do this, we can be present and available for our children—who so desperately need to know that their living parent is still here, and that they did not "lose" us too.

Our children watch our every move. The way we live is a demonstration to them. When we stumble, they watch how we respond. When we succeed, they watch the process. This doesn't mean we need to avoid all mistakes, but we get to decide how we engage with ourselves and the world around us. There is great power in how we choose to *live* our grieving.

Marni Henderson
Idaho, United States
Founder, Sunrise Retreats

Week 49

Danna Gildersleeve

Ready or not, life moves forward. It's been eight years missing my husband and feeling his absence on birthdays, holidays, and special occasions. While he is forever missed, my kids and I keep finding ways to take Dad along for the most precious moments.

My children were thirteen and sixteen when their dad passed, and each year on their birthday, I give them a gift from Dad which includes a memory of him written on his monogrammed stationery. For my son's eighth-grade graduation, he wore one of Dad's ties. Yes, it was too wide and out of fashion, but he had a piece of Dad with him. My daughter wore his service pin from work and tucked it inside her prom dress; a quiet nod, but Dad was there. At high school graduation, they taped a picture with Dad inside their graduation caps. For a potential wedding someday, I saved a blue tie (a "something blue") to wrap around my daughter's bridal bouquet, so Dad can be with her walking down the aisle. For my son, I'll make a pocket square using Dad's white dress shirt for his wedding day.

These are not grand gestures. They are simply ways of keeping Dad present which bring comfort. They help us feel closer to him rather than just missing him—because close is right where he'd want to be.

Danna Gildersleeve
Maryland, United States

Week 50

Lane Pease Hendricks

Realize that your children will process the death of their parent throughout their lives. This is not a one-and-done.

If they are very young when the parent dies, they can only process at that developmental age, so at different ages they may revisit their grief. They will need to talk about their feelings and may seek more information about the person and/or the death.

Keep an open dialogue and know that some of the behaviors they display, even many years later, may be grief reactions.

Look for bereavement organizations that have open-ended services or a trusted therapist they can return to through the years.

Lane Pease Hendricks
Georgia, United States
Author, *We Come Together As One: Helping Families Grieve, Share, and Heal the Kate's Club Way*
Director of programs and partnerships,
Kate's Club

Week 51

Kelsey Chittick

L osing someone we care about feels like a natural disaster. One minute, life is calm and familiar; the next, everything looks and feels totally different. No one wanted this, yet here we are: in a place we don't want to be, where the pain seems unbearable and unimaginable.

It is true that in this moment, you have control over very few things. Yet you do have one choice, and this choice can change the trajectory of your life. The one thing you control is how you react and respond to this experience. You get to choose who you want to be in the next days, weeks, months, and years.

Ask yourself, *Am I ready to do the hard and beautiful work that each of us is ultimately called to do?*

If the answer is yes, prepare to experience the hardest, and the most magical, time of your life. Miracles and angels, strangers and friends will rise up to meet you. You are not alone. And someday, you won't just be okay—you will be exceptional.

Remember, you are stronger than you think. It won't always be this hard.

Keep going.

Kelsey Chittick
California, United States
Author, *Second Half: Surviving Loss and Finding Magic in the Missing*
Host, *Moms Don't Have Time to Grieve Podcast*

Week 52

Elke Thompson

It's okay to be sad, but it's okay to be happy too.

I know it probably doesn't feel like it right now, but the time will come when little pockets of happiness creep back into your life—when you'll smile and laugh, and maybe even love again. And you'll feel a sudden pang of guilt, regardless of how old you are—three, eight, fifteen, thirty-four, or fifty-seven.

Please don't let it take over. You haven't "moved on." You just kept on moving, because you didn't have a choice. The hole in your heart doesn't get any smaller, but you can make the world around it bigger.

The psychologist Dr. Geoff Warburton once said, "We honor the dead more by choosing to live well." I couldn't agree more.

Elke Thompson
Scotland, United Kingdom
Speaker and children's book author
Is Daddy Coming Back in a Minute?
What Happened to Daddy's Body?
Is It Still OK to Have Cuddles?

Conclusion

Congratulations on getting through this whole book.

Phew.

So-called "widow brain" or "grief brain" is real, and many grieving people report that they are unable to focus on reading more than a few paragraphs, even if they were previously voracious readers.

So give yourself a pat on the back, or a big old hug.

Perhaps you've patiently read one reflection per week, and even journaled about the thoughts that came up for you. Or maybe you blasted through the entire book in one afternoon.

In any case, you did it. You finished.

Yay, you!

I hope that hearing directly from the other widowed parents on these pages has left you with one essential message: You are not alone.

You really aren't.

You may want to consider taking another step: finding ways to move from *feeling* a little less alone to actually *being* a little less alone.

Following are a few ideas to help you do just that.

Attend Camp Widow

One great way to connect with other widowed people is by attending Camp Widow.

No, it's not camping. Not even close.

It's more like a few days away with hundreds of your new widowed friends, connecting, listening to incredible speakers, attending workshops, and generally feeling a lot less alone. There's dancing, and yes, even laughing.

It feels like just yesterday that I was sitting at lunch on my first day of Camp Widow in San Diego, chatting with three others I'd just met. At the end of the final morning session, a few of us looked around and said to those who happened to be sitting nearby, "Hey, do you want to grab some food?" Since none of us had arrived knowing anyone, off we went together to a nearby restaurant. It wasn't long before one woman in the group was regaling the others with stories about, as she put it, *turning her late husband into a coconut tree*. He'd wanted his ashes buried in Hawaii, with said tree planted atop—and it turned out that wasn't such a simple feat.

Since then, I've often wondered what the diners at nearby tables thought upon overhearing *that* conversation.

In any case, do check out Camp Widow. They run programs a few times a year in various locations, and they serve people of any age, gender, or marital status who have lost their partners. See Appendix 1 for their website.

Find Local Grief Support

Many communities have grief centers or programs, which generally include groups for various ages of kids, including teens, and often they have groups for young adults, parents, and other adults as well. Some of the larger centers even have groups for specific types of loss, such as suicide, Covid, or cancer. They may have weekly or monthly groups, family nights, or grief camps. Some also offer individual or family sessions with counselors specializing in grief.

In addition to grief centers, you may be able to find local grief support groups through hospices (even if your family didn't use their services), cancer centers, or churches. If going online or calling around to find options sounds daunting, consider asking a friend to do the research for you. This can be a good task for someone who wants to help but isn't sure how.

You can search for a grief support program near you at the websites of the National Alliance for Children's Grief or Dougy Center, which you'll find in Appendix 1 along with a list of other terrific resources.

Seek out Other Widowed People in Your Community

Not all support must be formal in nature. Sometimes what you need is a group of widowed pals who just kind of "get it." It doesn't matter so much if your losses are from the same causes, if your kids are the same ages, or if you've been widowed similar lengths of time. What matters is that you're in the trenches of widowed parenting together, trying to figure out how to make sense of it all.

Many people don't know anyone in their personal circles who is also widowed and raising kids or teens.

Or rather, I'd suggest that they don't *realize* they know anyone.

If you were to start asking around, I bet

you'd find some people you could meet for coffee. Maybe it's a parent on your kid's soccer team who you've never really spoken with, your sister's neighbor, or your colleague's cousin. Try mentioning to friends and acquaintances that you're looking for other younger widowed folks to connect with, and I bet they will readily introduce you to those they know who might fit the bill.

Find a "Widow Buddy"

Once you've found a few other widowed parents—perhaps through Camp Widow, a local grief program, or your own outreach—why not become "widow buddies?"

Set an intention of getting together on a regular basis. That could look like dinners every Thursday at someone's house. Monthly happy hours out somewhere, so no one has to cook. If you have young kids, perhaps a standing playdate or park outing. You get the idea. Something easy, informal, and dare I say *fun*.

You may find it helpful to talk through some of the reflections and ideas in this book with your widow buddy. Why not send them a copy, with a little note of support? You can gift them an e-book—absolutely free—by visiting

WidowedParentInstitute.com/widowed-parents-unite-gift.

———

If none of these ideas for connecting with other widowed people feels feasible right now, I'd encourage you to keep taking smaller steps on your own, at home, in whatever pockets of time you can manage. Following are some suggestions.

Read Grief Memoirs

One of the best ways I've found to feel less alone is to read grief memoirs. When I interviewed Zibby Owens, author, publisher, and creator of the Moms Don't Have Time to Grieve community, she shared that one the reasons she loves reading memoirs is that it feels like sitting down for coffee with a friend who's going through some things, and learning from their struggles. In Appendix 3, you'll find a recommended list of some memoirs by widowed people. Some were written by those you've already met in the pages of this book. Even if an author's story is a little different from our own, reading memoirs is a great way for us to learn from one other.

Listen to Podcasts

Another great way to feel less alone is to listen to grief podcasts. Discussions can range from everyday people sharing their stories, to interviews with experts and authors, to well-known folks sharing their tips and reflections. I'm partial toward my own *Widowed Parent Podcast*, of course, where I interview widowed parents, people who lost a parent when they were young, and a variety of experts on topics of interest to those who are widowed and raising kids and teens. I hear from listeners all the time that they feel so much less alone after listening to others share their stories.

There are many other excellent grief podcasts too, and you'll find some more suggestions in Appendix 2.

Sign up for Fifty-Two Weeks of Tips and Prompts

If you've enjoyed the tips shared in this book by fellow widowed parents, you can sign up to receive one of them in your inbox every week for the next year.

Yes, they are the same tips found in this book.

But here's the thing: by getting them again,

spread out over fifty-two weeks, you'll have a chance to revisit them. Chances are they will land differently the next time around, because you'll likely be in a different place then. Some things may be easier, some harder, and different thoughts or ideas will probably be occupying your mind.

For me, when I re-encounter an idea or piece of writing that I first came across months or years earlier, it can elicit an entirely different understanding the second time around—just because I'm interpreting it through a new lens with the passage of time.

Plus, each weekly message comes with a journaling prompt. Journaling is optional, of course; you could instead discuss the question with your widowed friends, or your therapist, or ponder it while you're out walking (one of my favorite things to do). Or ignore the prompts all together, and just soak in the reflections your fellow widowed parents are sharing with you.

To get fifty-two weeks of tips in your inbox from your fellow widowed parents, visit WidowedParentInstitute.com/52tips.

—

As I said in the beginning of this book, there are—sadly—far too many of us widowed parents raising our kids and teens alone after our partners have died.

And like I mentioned, when I interview guests for the podcast, I always ask at the end: "If you could say one thing to widowed parents, what would it be?"

My own answer to that question is this: "Grief support" is like "swimming lessons."

What on earth is she talking about, you ask?

Here's what I mean: Swimming is a life skill. We teach our kids to swim as a preventative measure. A protective move. We don't wait until they are drowning to begin teaching them how to be safe around the water; we proactively sign them up for swimming lessons to help them learn the skills they'll need for a lifetime of exposure to aquatic environments.

So it is with grief. Healthy grieving, and coping in the face of losses large and small, is a life skill. If we live long enough (and here's hoping we do!), we will lose friends, neighbors, and colleagues—and yes, those closest to us, too. If we set our kids up with grief support now, they can learn some healthy grieving and coping skills early in life, which will serve them well both in the short term and throughout their lifetimes.

Psychologist J. William Worden, in his book *Grief Counseling and Grief Therapy (5th Edition)*, provides a framework he calls the "Tasks of Mourning." In it, he outlines the "four basic tasks" he feels are essential for a grieving person to address. They are:

Task 1: To accept the reality of the loss;
Task 2: To process the pain of grief;
Task 3: To adjust to a world without the deceased; and
Task 4: To find a way to remember the deceased while embarking on the rest of one's journey through life.

Just because the tasks are described as "basic" doesn't mean they are easy or quick. Neither are they linear. A grieving person might bounce around between them, focusing on one or two initially, then others, then back to the first ones again. Some tasks will certainly be harder than others. Some may initially seem impossible —and all of them will likely be unwelcome.

Participating in a grief support group can help kids (and adults!) begin to address these "Tasks of Mourning," and do so in a supportive environment. The structure and activities of grief support groups are designed to help participants learn healthy grieving and coping skills, and begin to integrate their losses into their lives.

In addition to doing this grief work, most kids and teens who lose a parent can benefit from connecting with peers whose parents have also died. Whether these young people are talking about grief, or not discussing it at all—perhaps playing together, laughing, or sharing a meal—being with other kids who "get it" can be comforting. Many kids report some level of awkwardness with their friends and classmates who have not experienced a loss, and it can be a relief to be in an environment where grief is normalized.

The bottom line is this: You don't have to wait for some threshold of struggling or suffering to seek grief support. You don't have to wait until someone is (metaphorically) drowning. There's no magic formula that says, "If I—or my kid—am struggling *this* much, then we need grief support. But not before then."

You can reasonably assume that if a kid has experienced the death of a parent, grief support is worth considering—and likely worth trying. I encourage you to seek out such support sooner rather than later. Worst case, your family checks it out and decide it's not for you.

And best case? You and your kids connect with other grieving families, learn some healthy grieving and coping skills, and begin to find your way forward in this world that you didn't choose, but in which you find yourselves none-theless.

—

I hope that the tips and reflections shared in this book will provide some small measure of comfort and help you feel ever-so-slightly less alone. Your fellow widowed parents are rooting for you.

From one widowed parent to another: you've got this.

Acknowledgments

Writing a book sometimes feels like a solitary undertaking, but it is most definitely not. Many hours of tapping the keyboard and staring at the ceiling must merge with a million collaborative and public activities to bring a book to publication and ensure it lands in the hands of the reader who needs it. Accordingly, I'd like to extend my thanks to the following incredible people:

To my guests on *The Widowed Parent Podcast*, past and future, thank you for sharing your journeys with my listeners, and for teaching us all so much.

To my fellow members of the National Alliance for Children's Grief and the NACG team, thank you for the vital work you're doing. Widowed parents need support with and for their children and you're doing so much for us. Keep up the great work.

To my colleagues who are dedicated and passionate writers, speakers, thinkers, and leaders in the wider grief world, thank you for the work you're each doing to make the world a better place. It's an honor to do this work along side you.

To AJ Harper and Laura Stone and the Author Club community, thank you for being there day in and day out as I've worked through the ups and downs of writing a book with forty-eight contributing authors. AJ, I've held the principles of your book *Write a Must-Read* firmly in mind as I shaped *Widowed Parents Unite*, and this book is better for it.

To Zibby Owens, thank you for being a supporter and champion of authors everywhere, and of this author in particular. I loved visiting with you when I was in New York, and hope to do so again before too much more time goes by.

To my colleagues in the Recognized Expert community, my former colleagues at IBM, my teachers and professors who helped shape my interest in learning and writing, and a lifetime of friends far and wide, thank you for influencing who I am today and how I show up in the world. Special shout-outs to Tammy Gooler Loeb, my original writing accountability buddy, podcast twin, and dear friend, and to Julie Lythcott-Haims and Melissa d'Arabian, who continue to inspire.

To Micki Burns, Charles Cobbs, Allison Gilbert, Julie Lythcott-Haims, BJ Miller, Buffy

Peters, Mary Robinson, Lauren Schneider, Leslie Gray Streeter, Gina Warner, and Justin Yopp, you'll always have a special place in my heart as endorsers of my first book, *Future Widow*. Jana DeCristofaro, your foreword sets up the book perfectly and brings such an important perspective to the work. Thank you all for extending kindness to this debut author and my deeply personal memoir.

To Cathy Callans, Hope Edelman, Joanne Harpel, Michele Neff Hernandez, Meghan Riordan Jarvis, Elena Lister, Ryan Loiselle, Gina Moffa, Karen Phelps Moyer, Claire Bidwell Smith, and Brennan Wood, thank you for your enthusiastic support and incredible endorsements for *Widowed Parents Unite*. I'm lucky to count you as colleagues and friends.

To Allison Gilbert, Barry Leiner Grant, Heidi Horsley, Herb Knoll, Emma Payne, and Brennan Wood, many thanks for helping me find additional contributing authors at a critical point in this project.

To Make Gallitelli, David Provolo, and Peya Robbins, thank you for your dedication and professionalism in your respective roles in bringing this book together. I appreciate you all. Special shout-out to Peya for embracing my long and sometimes rambling Voxers, and for your ongoing support and teamwork.

To Jocelyn Carbonara and Scott Carbonara, your editorial brilliance shines throughout this book. Thank you. I'm thrilled to call you both friends and colleagues.

To Azuráe Johnson Redmond, thank you for bringing your experience to my readers in the foreword of *Widowed Parents Unite*. It perfectly sets up the book and brings a powerful lens to the work. My deepest appreciation.

To the forty-eight contributing authors of *Widowed Parents Unite*, thank you for sharing your experiences and reflections with our readers. I know they will learn so much, and feel less alone because of what you've shared. I hope to meet you each in person one day.

To my family and friends near and far, including my local widowed friends, thank you for your continued support, cheerleading, and interest in my work. It means so much to me.

To Peter and Megan, thank you for allowing me the privilege of being your mom. You're the reason I do what I do.

To Dennis, thank you for the honor of being your wife. Your life was far too short; I promise to make the most of mine.

Appendix 1
Resources for Widowed Parents

Art with Heart: Workbooks & Journals for Kids
& Teens
https://artwithheart.org

Camp Kesem
https://www.kesem.org

Coping After Suicide
https://www.copingaftersuicide.com

The Dinner Party
https://www.thedinnerparty.org

Dougy Center: The National Center for
Grieving Children & Families
https://www.dougy.org

Eluna & Camp Erin
https://elunanetwork.org

EmpowerHER
https://www.empoweringher.org

For Grief
https://www.forgrief.com

Grief.com
https://grief.com

Hamilton's Academy of Grief and Loss
https://www.hamiltonsfuneralhome.com

Help Texts: SMS Text-Based Grief Support
https://helptexts.com/jennylisk

The Memory Circle
https://thememorycircle.com

Modern Loss
https://modernloss.com

Modern Widows Club
https://modernwidowsclub.org

Moms Don't Have Time to Grieve
https://www.instagram.com/momsdonthave-
timetogrieve

Motherless Daughters
https://hopeedelman.com

National Alliance for Children's Grief
https://childrengrieve.org

National Center for School Crisis &
Bereavement
https://www.schoolcrisiscenter.org

Open to Hope
https://www.opentohope.com

Outward Bound for Grieving Teens
https://www.outwardbound.org

Reimagine
https://letsreimagine.org

Soaring Spirits & Camp Widow
https://soaringspirits.org

Sunrise Retreats
https://sunriseretreat.org

TAPS (for Military Families)
https://www.taps.org

What's Your Grief
https://whatsyourgrief.com

The Widow Squad
https://widowsquad.com

Widowed Parent Institute
https://widowedparentinstitute.com

Widowed Parent Program
https://widowedparent.org

Widower's Support Network
https://widowerssupportnetwork.com

Young, Black & Widowed Inc.
https://www.youngblackwidowed.org

Appendix 2
Grief Podcasts

Conversations Between Widows

The Embracing Widowhood Podcast

Grief is My Side Hustle

Grief Out Loud

Moms Don't Have Time to Grieve

Open to Hope

Widow 180: The Podcast

The Widow Squad Podcast

The Widowed Parent Podcast

Appendix 3
Widow Memoirs

Available As Is: A Midlife Widow's Search for Love, by Debbie Weiss

Black Widow: A Sad-Funny Journey Through Grief for People Who Normally Avoid Books with Words Like "Journey" in the Title, by Leslie Gray Streeter

Filled with Gold: A Widow's Story, by Melissa Pierce

From Scratch: A Memoir of Love, Sicily, and Finding Home, by Tembi Locke

Future Widow: Losing My Husband, Saving My Family, and Finding My Voice, by Jenny Lisk

Kizuki: Life's Tidal Waves + Epiphanies = Love Beyond Time and Death, by Mae Yoshikawa (forthcoming)

An Obesity of Grief: A Journey from Traumatic Loss to Undying Love, by Lynn Haraldson

Second Half: Surviving Loss and Finding Magic in the Missing, by Kelsey Chittick

Shipwrecked: A Memoir on Widowed Parenting, by Jeanette Koncikowski (forthcoming)

Singing Beyond Sorrow: A Year of Grief, Gratitude, and Grace, by Carole Marie Downing

Widowish, by Melissa Gould

You Can't Do It Alone: A Widow's Journey Through Loss, Grief, and Life After, by Maria Quiban Whitesell

Appendix 4
Children's Books

El Alma Mágica, by Marisela Marquez

I Have a Question about Cancer: Clear Answers for All Kids, Including Children with Autism Spectrum Disorder or Other Special Needs, by Arlen Grad Gaines and Meredith Englander Polsky

I Have a Question about Death: Clear Answers for All Kids, Including Children with Autism Spectrum Disorder or Other Special Needs, by Arlen Grad Gaines and Meredith Englander Polsky

I Love You Always & Forever / Siempre te voy amar, by Marisela Marquez

The Invisible String, by Patrice Karst

Is Daddy Coming Back in a Minute?, by Elke Thompson

Is It Still OK to Have Cuddles?, by Elke Thompson

The Magical Soul, by Marisela Marquez

RIP Corey: My Friend Died and It Sucks, by Chris Buchanan

What Happened to Daddy's Body?, by Elke Thompson

Appendix 5
Other Grief Books

The AfterGrief: Finding Your Way Along the Long Arc of Loss, by Hope Edelman

Anxiety: The Missing Stage of Grief, by Claire Bidwell Smith

The Beauty of What Remains: How Our Greatest Fear Becomes Our Greatest Gift, by Steve Leder

A Beginner's Guide to the End, by BJ Miller and Shoshana Berger

Finding Peace, One Piece at a Time, by Rachel Kodanaz

Finding Meaning: The Sixth Stage of Grief, by David Kessler

For You When I Am Gone: Twelve Essential Questions to Tell a Life Story, by Steve Leder

For You When I Am Gone: A Journal: A Step-by-Step Guide to Writing Your Ethical Will, by Steve Leder

Giving Hope: Conversations with Children About Illness, Death, and Loss, by Elena Lister and Michael Schwartzman

Grief in the Workplace, by Rachel Kodanaz

Grieving Beyond Gender: Understanding the Ways Men and Women Mourn, by Kenneth Doka and Terry Martin

The Group: Seven Widowed Fathers Reimagine Life, by Donald Rosenstein and Justin Yopp

It's OK That You're Not OK: Meeting Grief and Loss in a Culture That Doesn't Understand, by Megan Devine

Living with Loss, One Day at a Time, by Rachel Kodanaz

The Modern Loss Handbook: An Interactive Guide to Moving Through Grief and Building Your Resilience, by Rebecca Soffer

Motherless Daughters: The Legacy Of Loss, by Hope Edelman

Moving On Doesn't Mean Letting Go: A Modern Guide to Navigating Loss, by Gina Moffa

Option B: Facing Adversity, Building Resilience, and Finding Joy, by Sheryl Sandberg and Adam Grant

Passed and Present: Keeping Memories of Loved Ones Alive, by Allison Gilbert

Second Firsts: A Step-By-Step Guide to Life After Loss, by Christina Rasmussen

Someone Died - Now What?: A Personal and Professional Perspective on Coping with Grief and Loss, by Corrie Sirota

Stepparenting the Grieving Child: Cultivating Past and Present Connections with Children Who Have Lost a Parent, by Diane Ingram Fromme

We Come Together As One: Helping Families Grieve, Share, and Heal the Kate's Club Way, by Lane Pease Hendricks and Nancy Kriseman

Welcome to the Grief Club: Because You Don't Have to Go Through It Alone, by Janine Kwoh

What's Your Grief?: Lists to Help You Through Any Loss, by Eleanor Haley and Litsa Williams

A Widow's Guide to Healing, by Kristin Meekhof

Appendix 6
Parenting Books

The Addiction Inoculation: Raising Healthy Kids in a Culture of Dependence, by Jessica Lahey

The Effort Myth: How to Give Your Child the Three Gifts of Motivation, by Sherri Fisher

The Emotional Lives of Teenagers: Raising Connected, Capable, and Compassionate Adolescents, by Lisa Damour

The Gift of Failure: How the Best Parents Learn to Let Go So Their Children Can Succeed, by Jessica Lahey

Grown and Flown: How to Support Your Teen, Stay Close as a Family, and Raise Independent Adults, by Lisa Heffernan and Mary Dell Harrington

How to Be a Happier Parent: Raising a Family, Having a Life, and Loving (Almost) Every Minute, by KJ Dell'Antonia

How to Raise an Adult: Break Free of the Overparenting Trap and Prepare Your Kid for Success, by Julie Lythcott-Haims

Middle School Matters: The 10 Key Skills Kids Need to Thrive in Middle School and Beyond - and How Parents Can Help, by Phyllis Fagell

Middle School Superpowers: Raising Resilient Tweens in Turbulent Times, by Phyllis Fagell

Soundbite: The Admissions Secret that Gets You Into College and Beyond, by Sara Harberson

Under Pressure: Confronting the Epidemic of Stress and Anxiety in Girls, by Lisa Damour

Untangled: Guiding Teenage Girls Through the Seven Transitions into Adulthood, by Lisa Damour

Your Turn: How to Be an Adult, by Julie Lythcott-Haims

Appendix 7
More for Readers

If you've enjoyed the tips shared in this book by fellow widowed parents, you can sign up to receive one of them in your inbox every week for the next year. Plus, each weekly message comes with a prompt, perfect for journaling or discussing with your widow buddy.

To get fifty-two weeks of tips in your inbox from your fellow widowed parents, visit WidowedParentInstitute.com/52tips.

Does your widow buddy have a copy of this book? If not, why not send them a copy, along with a little note of support? You can gift them an e-book—absolutely free—by visiting WidowedParentInstitute.com/widowed-parents-unite-gift.

For more tips and resources, please visit WidowedParentInstitute.com/widowed-parent-resources.

Finally, are your friends wondering how to support you? Send them to WidowedParentInstitute.com/grief-allies.

The Widowed Parent Podcast

Guiding the Journey of
Solo Parenting After Loss

Experiencing the profound loss of a spouse while navigating the intricate realm of "only-parenting" is a challenge unlike any other. Remember, though, you're not journeying alone. Jenny Lisk, who stepped into solo parenting following the devastating loss of her husband to brain cancer, established the Widowed Parent Institute to shine a light, extend a hand, and share vital resources. The Widowed Parent Podcast embodies that commitment, providing a mix of hope, practical wisdom, and shared experiences.

On The Widowed Parent Podcast, you'll find:

- Expert perspectives from the vanguard of grief and loss research, tailored distinctly for widowed parents.
- Heartfelt stories from those who walked through childhood after the

death of a parent, granting unique perspective and hope.
- Candid conversations with widowed parents, unveiling both the strengths they've discovered and the hurdles they've faced.

Whether you're trying to connect with a young child's emotions, navigate the maze of teenage years, or simply seeking a community that truly understands, this podcast speaks directly to widowed parents of children at every stage, from infancy through college. Plug in during a peaceful walk, your daily commute, or in quiet reflection, and discover inspiration, empowerment, and a community that hears and understands.

Proudly presented by the Widowed Parent Institute, a beacon of practical guidance, invaluable resources, and steadfast support for mothers and fathers raising grieving children and teens. Available on Spotify, Apple Podcasts, YouTube, and wherever you get your podcasts.

The Widowed Parent Podcast
"Start Here" Playlist on Spotify:
widowedparentinstitute.com/start-here-spotify

Also by Jenny Lisk

Future Widow Excerpt © 2021
Reprinted by Permission

When you finally arrive home on a Friday evening--one kid in tow, the other successfully deposited with the Boy Scouts for the weekend--and your forty-something-year old husband has a funny look on his face, your first thought is unlikely to be:

This time next year I'll be a widow, raising two grieving kids alone.

At least, that certainly was not *my* first thought.

After fighting the cross-town traffic charac-teristic of Seattle's suburbs, I got home one night to find Dennis sitting on the couch in our living room. He had a *look* on his face. I can't really describe it, except to say it was that look that said something was wrong.

The sort of look you recognize after sixteen years of marriage.

I thought something had happened at work, or maybe some thing else had gone wrong that day. My read of his face was more "pissed off" than "terminally ill."

"What's up?" I asked, my measured tone belying my concern.

"I've been feeling a little dizzy lately."

I sat down on the couch and peppered him with questions.

What are you noticing? When did it start? How often are you feeling dizzy?

He described some slight and occasional dizziness over the previous few days. Nothing dramatic. No I-can't-stand-up moments. No blacking out; nothing that would ring alarm bells.

Since it was after hours, going to see his regular doctor wasn't an option. Nothing about the situation suggested I needed to take him to the emergency room, or even to urgent care. We decided that Dennis should call his doctor on Monday, and we talked about times when I could go in with him.

Somehow, my tagging along seemed like it could be important. Little did I know how true my hunch would prove to be.

Within two weeks, I would become his full-time caregiver.

For more information or to purchase, please visit futurewidowbook.com.

About the Author

Jenny Lisk is the founder of the Widowed Parent Institute. She is an award-winning author and widowed mom who is dedicated to helping widowed parents increase their family's well-being.

In her memoir, *Future Widow*, Jenny draws on her personal and professional experience to provide a real-life guide for surviving and thriving while raising grieving children.

As host of *The Widowed Parent Podcast*, Jenny has done more than 150 interviews with experts, seasoned widowed parents, and people who lost a parent at a young age. Her podcast guides the journey of solo parenting after loss.

Jenny lives in Redmond, Washington, with her two teenagers. Please visit her website at jennylisk.com and connect with her on social media @liskjenny.